Essential Skills for a Brillia

Book 2

Leave It!

How to teach Amazing Impulse Control
to your Brilliant Family Dog

Beverley Courtney

Books by the author

Essential Skills for a Brilliant Family Dog

Book 1 Calm Down! *Step-by-Step to a Calm, Relaxed, and Brilliant Family Dog*

Book 2 Leave It! *How to teach Amazing Impulse Control to your Brilliant Family Dog*

Book 3 Let's Go! *Enjoy Companionable Walks with your Brilliant Family Dog*

Book 4 Here Boy! *Step-by-step to a Stunning Recall from your Brilliant Family Dog*

Essential Skills for your *Growly* but Brilliant Family Dog

Book 1 Why is my Dog so Growly? *Teach your fearful, aggressive, or reactive dog confidence through understanding*

Book 2 Change for your Growly Dog! *Action steps to build confidence in your fearful, aggressive, or reactive dog*

Book 3 Calm walks with your Growly Dog *Strategies and techniques for your fearful, aggressive, or reactive dog*

www.brilliantfamilydog.com/books

Free Training for you!

Jumping up?
Barking?
Chewing?

Get inventive solutions to everyday problems with your dog

www.brilliantfamilydog.com

Disclaimer

I have made every effort to make my teachings crystal clear, but we're dealing with live animals here (That's you, and your dog.) and I can't see whether you're doing it exactly right. I am unable to guarantee success, as it depends entirely on the person utilising the training programs, strategies, tools, and resources.

What I do know is that this system works!

Nothing in these books should upset or worry your dog in any way, but if your dog has a pre-existing problem of fear or aggression you should consult a force-free trainer to help. www.brilliantfamilydog.com/growly will get you started.

By the way, to simplify matters I refer to our trainee dog throughout this series as "she." "He" and "she" will both learn the exact same way. The cumbersome alternatives of "he/she" or "they" depersonalise our learner: I want her to be very real to you!

All the photos in this book are of "real" dogs – either my own, or those of students and readers (with their permission). So the reproduction quality is sometimes not the best. I have chosen the images carefully to illustrate the concepts – so we'll have to put up with some fuzziness.

Contents

Introduction
Now you see it, now you don't

Gunner waits politely in front of a handful of cheese and sausage

"I only turned my back for a second," Sally wailed to me in class, "and the whole cake was gone!"

She'd left it on the kitchen worktop, out of reach of her dog Jacko - or so she thought! She came back from her phone call to see the dog in his bed, his face festooned with frosting, polishing off the last remains of the cake.

This thieving happened regularly, which showed that Sally was a bit of a slower learner than Jacko!

For some dogs it's "counter-surfing" - stealing food from the kitchen worktops. For others, it's anything they can snatch up from the floor. It could be the children's toys, stones from the drive, or ice cream from a child's hand.

Oh, and don't forget dead things they find on country walks which will make them sick on the carpet later.

There's also the safety issue of sharp things, poisonous things, and medications. It could be jumping out of the car as soon as the door is opened a crack, crashing through doors at home, barging past you on the stairs to trip you up, or leaping about like a thing possessed when you mention the word "walk". Then there's barking at the window, yipping at other dogs playing, and whining for dinner.

All stem from the same issue - lack of impulse control.

See it - gotta have it!

We have no problem teaching our children how to control their desires - so why do we struggle with dogs? Perhaps people tend to think they can't expect anything better. "It's only a dog," they tell themselves. As you probably know if you've reared children or managed staff - *what you expect is what you get!*

Dogs can learn just as well as children can. In the wild, they would need to learn self-control in order to survive in a competitive environment. Puppies learn early not to interfere with big brother's dinner, and organising a hunt can involve days of hunger, stalking, and patience. In their natural state, dogs are opportunist scavengers. A whole cake just above nose level? Obviously a prize for the dog.

There isn't a moral issue here. Until you teach her what's what, any food is fair game for your dog.

Dogs don't do things to spite their owners! Dogs do what works.

If swiping the cake off the counter tastes good, then they'll do it again and again. Why shouldn't they? But it doesn't mean that your house has to be in permanent lockdown for the next fifteen years.

- Would you like to be able to leave food out wherever you want, secure in the knowledge that your dog won't touch it?
- Would you like to have a dog who sits calmly to have the lead put on when you're getting ready for a walk?
- How about waiting at the top of the stairs to be released, rather than charging down to trip you up?
- Keeping their feet on the floor when visitors arrive?
- Or leaving those tasty and dangerous slugs and pebbles well alone?

I hear you thinking, "This must involve loads of different training techniques. I'll be forever training my dog new things when all I want is a companion dog and a quiet life!"

Nope. It's just the one thing: *Impulse Control.*

It was having to learn the techniques to make a Brilliant Family Dog with my own busy household of multiple dogs, cats, sheep, goats, hens, and children that set me on the road to helping others do the same. I learnt early on that forcing someone to do something only resulted in grudging compliance at best; whereas getting them to participate and enjoy the process turned them into eager and fast learners. This applied equally to the dogs, the goats - and the children! The sheep and the cats not so much.

My qualifications range from the understanding of learning theory to specialist work for fearful, anxious, and growly dogs. Acquiring an anxious, growly dog of my own ensured that I learnt and understood the process of assimilating the dog into our world in a way which builds her confidence.

There are some superb teachers and advocates of force-free dog training, and you'll find those I am particularly indebted to in the Resources section at the end of this book. Some of the methods I'll be showing you are well-known in the force-free dog training community, while many have my own particular twist.

My work revolves around puppies, new rescue dogs, growly dogs - and, of course, dog owners. There are many people more gifted than I who can train animals to do astonishing things. My gift lies in being able to convey my knowledge to the dog's caregiver in a way which has them saying, "It's so obvious when you put it like that!"

Dogs are individuals and so are their owners, so sometimes creativity and imagination are needed to solve a problem. There isn't a one-size-fits-all approach to training - as you'll see when you look at the Troubleshooting sections following the lessons in the book.

I suggest you read the whole book before you start so you yourself are clear what you need and what you are aiming for. Then re-read the lesson you're working on and go straight into your very short session. After this you can assess where you are and check the Troubleshooting section for any difficulties that relate to you and your dog. Then you're ready for your next session the next day.

Chapter 1
It's all about choice

Lacy's self-control is sorely tested!

Wouldn't you like your dog to make the right choice without having to be told every time? This is how we bring up children. Take toothbrushing, for example. To begin, we have to brush our children's teeth for them, then we move to telling them to do it. As they get a bit older, we ask them if they've remembered to do it. Eventually (I see wry smiles from the parents amongst you!) we stop altogether and they do it by themselves.

This is what we are aiming to accomplish with your dog.

Dogs are simple souls. They do what works. They operate entirely on consequences. For instance, if they get lots of tasty morsels when they raid the bin, they'll do it again. If they raid the bin and get their head stuck and cut their tongue on a tin, then they may not attempt it again! If they raid the bin and it's empty - or full of non-food items - they'll probably try again another time. If they've successfully raided the bin before, and this time it's empty, then they'll keep trying until they get something - or till they're satisfied that the bin is always empty.

This is a bit like us with a one-armed bandit: people don't leave after a payout. They keep trying till they run out of money then leave, dispirited.

Your dog is making choices all the time. We just want to direct her to make the choices we like.

What will this mean for your dog?

- No more mysterious tellings-off for breaking rules she didn't know existed
- More freedom!
- More companionship with you around the house
- More outings with you
- More affection and appreciation from you

What will this mean for you?

- No more shouting
- No barking commands which your dog doesn't understand
- No firefighting - trying too late to change something your dog is doing
- The comfort of trust
- Companionship (why did you get your dog in the first place?)
- Peace and harmony in the home

Choices, choices

In training, the simplest way to get the dog to choose is by – you've guessed it! - offering her a choice. This may appear totally obvious when you think about it, but if you go the other way, and continually limit her choices, she'll never learn what you want to teach her.

Sometimes it doesn't matter to you which she chooses, like when you ask her, "Do you want to play with your ball or your frisbee?" Sometimes it matters a lot, and you'll weight the choices so she's most likely to choose what you want.

Here's a quick example of weighting the choices, you offer to put her lead on. If she sits, you put it on. If she jumps about crazily, you put it away again. There isn't any need for shouting or dancing about! Both of those actions are going to wind up your dog as well as you, and are not going to achieve the outcome you want. It will lead to frustration all round and a breakdown in communication between the two of you.

Give your dog a choice, and *wait* for her to choose what action to take.

In the example of you offering her lead, the reward for sitting still to have the lead put on is going out for a walk. If she leaps about and yodels, you can simply and silently put the lead back where it lives, then sit down and read a book.

After a bit of puzzlement your dog will probably come and stare at you. She's trying to work this out. When you're ready, you can fetch the lead again. Hold it in front of you and *wait*. Is your dog a little calmer this time round? No? Put the lead away and go back to your book. Let the dog settle down.

Now try again. Hold the lead and *wait*.

By now your dog should have worked out that what she was doing before was not working, and she's ready to try something different. As soon as she stands still for a moment (a Sit is not necessary at this stage) and is quiet, you can tell her how good she is, put the lead on, and head out for the walk. You can gradually wait for a sit, a silent sit, a silent still sit, a silent still sit for the time it takes you to get your coat on, and so on, until the sight of the lead causes your dog to sit and wait patiently for the inevitable walk.

But before she can do that, she has to know that what *she* does affects what *you* do.

If you don't give her a choice it'll be pot luck whether she ever works it out. Giving her a choice, showing her that her actions affect outcomes, gives her a responsibility that she will grow into. This will change your relationship for both of you. Rather than a master-robot relationship, you will have a friend-companion relationship. Much easier, much calmer, and much more fun!

Special equipment you'll need to teach Impulse Control

You'll be glad to know that there isn't any special equipment needed for these lessons! Just your usual dog-gear, though we'll have a quick look at what works best.

- A soft collar - fit it as loose as possible but without her being able to wriggle backwards and pull it over her ears. A soft webbing collar is good. I prefer one that is minutely adjustable and with a snap fastening. You can also use a buckle collar, though these are harder to adjust in the small increments needed for a puppy or small dog as you're stuck with the pre-defined holes.

- A 6-foot lead - one that is soft on your hands. If you need control when you're off-road, you can use a 15-foot soft long line.

- And if you want to use a harness, be sure that it's one you'd be comfortable in if you were wearing it!

Equipment you do NOT want to use

There is a lot of equipment on the market that is not suitable for the kind of interactions you are going to want with your dog. What I mean by that is any kind of aversive equipment - things that work by tightening, strangling, cutting, poking, shocking, and jabbing - and things that don't allow communication between the two of you.

In other words, don't use anything made of chain or spikes or operated with a battery. Also avoid extendable leads, bungee leads, and harnesses that operate by cutting up under the armpits.

How to reward your dog for her brilliant self-control

You will need to be able to reward your dog whenever she does something you like.

You'll need:

- A selection of toys your dog absolutely loves. Balls on ropes; soft tug toys made of fleece, sheepskin, or rabbit skin; and teddy bear-type toys - are all good.
- Mega-desirable treats! This means treats that your dog will sell her soul for, not dry kibble or pocket fluff as a rule. You can get some first-class commercial treats if you hunt carefully, but the best treats tend to be home-prepared, soft, slippery, flavoursome, smelly, and small.

The treats need to be very tasty - your dog has got to really want them! You don't want her chewing and chomping on a biscuit for so long that she forgets what she earnt it for! The treat needs to slip down quickly and make your dog think, "Wow! How can I get some more of that?" Your dog needs to know what you like and what does not cut it with you. Every time she does something you like, you can mark it by saying, "YES!" and giving her a treat.

Good treats

- Cheese
- Sausage
- Ham
- Chicken
- Frankfurter
- Salami
- Homemade sardine, tuna, or ham cookies
- Freeze-dried 100% meat treats
- Dehydrated liver, heart, lung, etc

…real food in other words. Ideally, they slip down quickly so your dog wants more. Cut them up into small, pea-size treats.

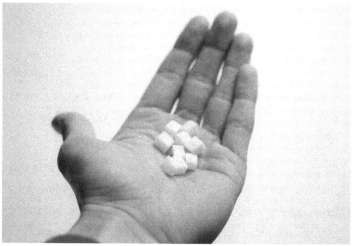

A handful of tasty little cheese treats

OK treats

- High-quality grain-free commercial treats

Fairly rubbish treats

- Your dog's usual kibble (She gets it anyway. Why should she have to work for it?)
- Cat biscuits
- Dog biscuits
- Stuff of unrecognisable composition sold as pet treats
- Anything you wouldn't put in your own mouth

Do you work more enthusiastically for £60 an hour or for 50p an hour? Quite so. Your dog is the same. Be sure the treats you're offering are worth working for.

Once you have these things in place, we're ready to get going with teaching your dog impulse control. You will probably be amazed at what your dog can do, and you will discover hitherto unknown depths to her personality. Let's get started!

In this Chapter we have established:

- Your dog needs to be given a choice to make a choice
- Your dog needs to be free to make mistakes and find out what works
- The importance of the right tools and the right treats
- "I like these new tasty treats! What do I have to do to get them?"

Chapter 2
Introducing the Magic Hand

Coco at 16 weeks admiring my lunch

You're going to teach your dog to control her impulses without shouting - or even speaking! You're going to work calmly and wait for her to figure out the game you're playing. Remember, your goal is to have her make a good choice all by herself.

Choose a quiet time, when you know your dog is hungry and not too tired. Prepare your treats and sit in a chair.

Lesson 1 Teaching the Magic Hand Game

1. Take a few of those tasty, flavourful, and strongly scented treats

2. Hold your hand out to your dog to show her what you have

3. As soon as she moves her nose forward to take the treats, close your fingers to hide the tasty snack

4. Keep your fist closed, fingers facing up, at dog-nose level. This is not a game of chase-the-hand, so keep your hand still. Now exercise your own impulse control by waiting.

5. Your dog will sniff, lick, poke, paw, and nuzzle at your hand. She may nibble your fingers. Let her.

6. If she really hurts you, you can say, "Ow", take your hand away for a moment, then put it back.

7. Carry on waiting while your dog pokes, sniffs, licks and nibbles. This will take as long as it takes - maybe several minutes for a determined thief.

8. At some stage she will stop digging at your fist. She will move her head away from your hand, and when she does, immediately open your fist to expose the food and close it again just as fast - before she dives in. Keep doing this every time she gives you a bit of space.

9. Your dog is discovering that moving away makes the hand open while being too close keeps the hand closed. Once she figures this new part of the game out, it's only a hop to discovering that staying away keeps the hand open!

10. Now watch your dog carefully. Dogs give different signs that they are waiting: some will lie down and stare at your hand, some will back away, some will sit and stare at you, some will turn their head right

away. Whatever sign your dog gives to show that she wants the food but that she's not going to try and snatch it, will take you to the next step. (If she just loses interest and wanders off, common in puppies, just make a kissy noise or touch her lightly to get her attention back to the task. We want distance, but we want her to stay engaged.)

11. While your dog keeps her polite distance, keep your cupped hand still, and slowly - with your other hand - take one treat and bring it towards her."Slowly" because we want to give her the chance to make a mistake. If she stays still, give her the treat, congratulating her warmly. If she lunges forward to meet it, drop it back in your hand, and close your fingers over it again. Just like us, dogs learn through their mistakes. Very soon she'll suss it out and stay rigidly still while you pass her a treat

12. Keep going with this sequence daily till your dog sees your fist in front of her nose and immediately backs off, sits, lies down, turns away, or gives whatever her sign is to show she's waiting. Once she gives the sign and stays still, you can slowly give her a treat with your other hand.

Many people are amazed the first time they run through this to find that their dog - however greedy she may usually be - can control herself and wait politely. Isn't this fun!

Impulse control is very much what we expect from our children, not to mention adults! When we put a plate of cakes on the table, we don't expect our visitors to dive on them and shovel them into their mouths. We expect them to wait patiently till we offer them a cake, then they put out their hand - without sticking their face in the plate - and take just one cake. You can expect the exact same manners from your dog.

Surprised?

Good! There are many more surprises on the way for you.

Troubleshooting

My dog tries for a while then wanders off.

Make sure your treats are highly desirable. I always like to know the treats I'm using are a personal favourite of whichever dog I'm working with. Remember, every dog is an individual. Choose a quiet time to start. Have her on a loose lead and tread or kneel on the lead to keep her from wandering too far. Persevere! It's important that you have impulse control and patience as well!

Ow! That hurts! My dog is scrabbling at my hand with his sharp claws!

Try holding your hand a little higher - right at nose level - to dissuade so much pawing. You can also clip and file his claws before your next session!

This seems to take forever.

Some dogs can take a while before they make the connection. Choose a quiet place to work. And keep going. Your dog needs to learn the consequence of her actions. We want her to know that she can get the treats when she cracks the code.

When I give her the treat from my hand she guzzles the whole lot.

Wait - you are picking up one treat and offering it with your other hand, right? Your dog never gets to put her nose in the treat-hand. She has to wait politely to be offered one treat, just like your visitor keeping a polite distance when offered the plate of cakes.

She seems to have got this, but when I tell her to sit she ignores me.

Don't tell her to sit - or anything else. We're looking for just one thing here: your dog controlling her natural impulse to grab any food in front of her. Telling her to sit is muddying the waters. You don't need to speak at all, though you can always tell your dog how brilliant she is, of course!

My dog doesn't seem to know what's wanted. He just sits there looking baffled.

Try to make the game more active, faster, and more exciting. You can also start off by giving him one of these amazing treats, so now he'll want to get more. As soon as he is not actively attacking your hand, you may open it so he can see the treats. Shut it fast. Open it. Shut it fast. If you have always told your dog what to do, or more likely what not to do, he may be waiting for direction from you. Stay silent, and let him see that he can make choices all on his own! We want the dog to try things, to see what works.

What do you mean by "engaged"?

Good question! I mean that your dog is totally involved in this game. She has bright eyes, cocked ears, swishing tail, and quick movements while she tries different ways to get the food. If she is "disengaged" she may be wandering off looking for something else to do, sniffing the floor, her movements slow. She may also be anxious as she's not sure what it is you want her to do. Anxiety will show up as yawning, avoiding eye contact, lip-licking, or lying down. If your dog is really worried and unhappy about playing with you, choose a better time and better treats, and encourage her attempts by using your voice. Don't make it easier or she won't learn anything! Make the game fun for your dog - it's a puzzle for her to solve.

My dog isn't that interested in food.

All dogs - indeed all animals - are interested in food. They have to have this drive or they'd die of starvation. So you need to set things up for success. Be sure your dog is hungry and has not eaten very recently. Get mega-super-incredible treats that smell intoxicating. A friend of mine calls them, "crack cocaine cookies"! The treats need to smell intoxicating to your dog, not to you - you may not be quite so enamoured of the smell of sardines or liver. If he's still not taking the treats, this indicates that he's too anxious and unsettled to work for you. Find out what's troubling him in the environment before you try again.

My dog is confused. I've been teaching her Hand Targets, so she thinks she should be bopping my hand with her nose!

Have a look at exactly what you do with your hand when you invite a Hand Target. Make sure your hand gestures are quite different for this game. You may, for instance, often be standing to teach Hand Targets, so you can sit and rest your arm on your knee for this lesson. Don't work them both in the same training session. Hand Targets are usually fairly active and fast. Your impulse control game will be quieter, more thoughtful. Be clear and your bright dog will work it out.

This seems too simple. As soon as she moves her face from my hand I give her a treat?

It is simple - yes! - but you've made it a bit too simple, and you're missing your greatest teaching opportunity. Once your dog pulls away from your closed hand, you open the hand. It's staying away from the treats in the open hand that's really hard! You need to wait for her to cue you that she is waiting. As soon as she's positively staying away you can then move to Step 11.

How on earth will this stop her chasing squirrels?

I'm glad you're thinking more broadly. Squirrels? That's food on the move. Once you've started to develop your dog's impulse control you'll be able to generalise it to other things. This will come later in the program. Get this part going first. We want to embed this in her subconscious so that the ability to resist becomes easy for her.

This last question is a useful segue into the next section:

How will this help with everyday grabbing and stealing?

To start with, we're focussing on food, which is the prime mover for most dogs and the easiest way to get very quick results. For now, you'll be able to proof your dog against

- Countersurfing - snaffling food off the kitchen worktops
- Cake on the coffee table
- Roast beef on the dinner table
- Sandwiches on the picnic rug
- Remains of the takeaway in the bin
- Dead rat in the hedge
- Biscuit in a child's hand
- Intercepting food on its way to your mouth
- Begging

We'll add a vocal cue to her action of turning away from temptation later on when she's doing it perfectly every time. For now you can use your Magic Hand to stop food attacks - there's no need to say anything. Instead of yelling, "*Oh no, the dog's about to eat the cake!*", causing universal panic and rushing to grab the dog, simply put your hand in front of the desired object and wait silently.

Your dog - if well-schooled in the sequence you worked on in the first lesson, the Magic Hand - will say, "Oops. Oh yeah, not for me," and back off.

What do you do then? Tell her off for trying to attack the cake? Send her out of the room for being a "bad dog"? NO! *She made a good choice* (albeit with a little help from your Magic Hand). You reward her! "What a good girl! Here's a treat for you," is what you'll be saying. Now she remembers how she can earn rewards from you.

Life becomes simpler

As you can see, this process shifts the choice to your dog. We are no longer dealing with a robotic dog who needs to be directed and commanded every moment of the day. *Your dog is taking responsibility for her own actions.* Once she's able to make a choice, she is involved in the process, rather than being a victim. You'll be seeing in the following chapters how to achieve this happy state for everything you expect of your dog.

In this Chapter we have established:

- How to start to teach your dog impulse control
- Lots of everyday problems will evaporate
- Life will become much easier!
- "I get loads of cheese!"

Chapter 3
Keeping away from dropped
or found food on the ground

*Oops! I dropped a waffle, but it's quite safe from
Cricket without me having to say a word*

By now you've been working the game in the last section for several days, and your dog knows the Magic Hand. When you offer your hand with treats in to her she says, "Ha! I know this game: you can't catch *me!*" This is the playful attitude you should be aiming for. This is a game. This isn't a way of stopping your dog doing something. It's a way of involving your dog in your life and allowing her to make a choice. All you have to do is be patient and ready with a handsome reward for the right decision.

Making the right choice will become more rewarding to your dog than scarfing up the food she's found.

That's been scientifically proven. Finding food will become an opportunity for her to perform her party trick, and gain a reward plus your pleasure and attention. Locating food will trigger the reward centres in the brain, even without getting the food.

Now we're going to move the game forward and look at teaching your dog to leave food on the floor.

This will include:

- Dropped food
- Found food
- Plate or cup on the floor in the living room
- Stolen food (if you weren't watching!)
- Disgusting yucky dead thing found on a walk - which will end up regurgitated on your bed
- Disgusting leftovers in town from last night's street carousing - resulting in more carpet-cleaning
- Dangerous substances or objects on the street
- Slugs, snails, pebbles, rubber bands
- Spilt chips outside the takeaway shop
- Something so rank that your dog can't decide whether to eat it or roll in it

The principle of this game is the same as in the first game - it's all about waiting for your dog to work the problem out and show self-control, without us telling her to do anything. But there is one major difference when working with food on the floor.

I never let my dogs have the food that they're keeping away from.

Once my dogs see anything on the ground, it's history. I will reward them for leaving it, but they'll never get it.

Many people teach their dog a sequence of "leave it - geddit!" with food on the floor. Dogs are great at anticipation - think of the sheepdog who sees one ewe twitch her ear in the wrong direction and he's round the outside of her like a shot, to herd her back in before she's been able to escape the flock. The Leave it - Geddit sequence will naturally become shorter and shorter, until your dog thinks, "I just have to stare at the food for a moment, then it's *mine*, mwah-ha-ha!"

Eating something found on the ground can have tragic results. The reason my dogs never get it is twofold:

1. Safety

- If I drop a bottle of pills - and the pills fly all over the place - I don't want my dog thinking he can just stare at them for a moment then start hoovering. Many of our over-the-counter medications are dangerous or deadly to dogs, never mind prescription drugs.
- It could be a packet of mince pies that has "fallen off" the kitchen counter, or perhaps someone's left the baking cupboard open and she's found the raisins - both are highly toxic to many dogs.
- Maybe you drop a box of chocolates or leave chocolate lying about. This too can land your dog in the vet's intensive care unit.
- You may come across some drug paraphernalia hidden on the street
- Slugs and snails can carry flukes and worms into your dog
- All told, what your dog finds on the ground is best left there

2. They can pass it by without demur

If they never get the thing they've located on the ground, then they won't bother looking for things on walks, and they won't expect you to do something with the found thing. Mine know that they get rewarded for pointing it out to me if I haven't spotted it myself. "Yes, it's a maggoty dead rat. Thank you for showing me - here's your treat." No need to haul your dog away from the prize. Life has just become a bit easier. Again.

Lesson 2 Teaching the Food-on-the-Floor Game, or Magic Hand 2.0

Once your dog has mastered the first Magic Hand Game, teaching this one is simplicity itself.

1. Take just two of those tasty, flavourful, and strongly scented treats, holding one in each hand.

2. Hold one hand out to your dog to show her what you have, then whap the treat onto the floor right in front of her, instantly covering it with your Magic Hand.

3. Keeping your hand still, palm down, you now exercise your own impulse control again by waiting.

4. Your dog will sniff, nuzzle and paw at your hand. Let her.

5. At some stage she will move away from your hand. Immediately lift your hand to expose the food, then slam it down over the tasty treat again just as fast - before she dives in. Keep doing this every time she gives you a bit of space. Huzzah! Your dog has just discovered that moving away makes the hand lift - it's the same game!

6. "I know this game!" She'll take up her accustomed position - backing off, lying down, staring at the food, sitting staring at you, turning her head away, or whatever she does with the Magic Hand Game - most importantly, she waits, tail wagging madly, while the defenceless treat lies on the floor in front of her.

7. Scoop up the first treat and give her the one from your other hand

with jubilation and enthusiasm for her cleverness.

8. Work on this game frequently, for just one cycle. You can gradually develop the game so that you can leave the first treat on the floor when she backs off, while you give her the second from your other hand. Then remove the first treat.

Troubleshooting

Ow! My dog is scrabbling at the back of my hand with her claws!

If you've worked sufficiently through the Magic Hand Game you shouldn't be getting scrabbling or scratching now. Go back and consolidate the first game so that she pulls away from your fist immediately, without nagging or mugging it.

This won't work for me: I toss treats on the floor in training.

So do I! It's a great way to get active training games going with your dog and to re-position them. They know the difference. I use a marker word before treating, so they know the tossed treat is for them, and the food is thrown within the context of a game we're playing. In the Food-on-the-Floor Game and Magic Hand Game you are offering your dog a choice. She needs to make the decision whether this food is for her or not. Mistakes are good, but confusion is not! Make sure your set-up is different and deliberate while she learns - possibly in a different part of the house.

My dog's backing off but only a little. When I lift my hand, her nose is only an inch from the treat, so she grabs it.

Wait her out. When she backs off a smidgin, uncover the food and cover it again fast! Speed is essential in this game. After a few times she'll realise that her nose is in danger, and that this is not working, so she'll back up a bit more. When she's drawn herself back to a polite distance that allows you to expose the treat without risk of it being scarfed up, you can give her your other treat.

My puppy lies down, so she's right on the treat.

When you first start this game your puppy may lie down by walking her front legs forward so she ends up too close to the treat. Just slide your hand-and-treat combo a little further away and continue the game. We're aiming for success, and if her nose is too close, it will be very hard for her.

Lesson 3 Bringing the game to real life!

Got Magic Hand 2.0 going well? Excellent! Now we can take it further and proof your dog against all things on the ground. Don't worry if your dog's toys are usually on the floor - we'll come to toys later. She can still play with them!

1. Drop a treat near your foot - be ready to cover it with your foot if your dog dives for it. This is the same gig - cover, uncover, cover, uncover - till your dog backs off, when you remove the treat on the ground and reward her with the treat in your other hand.

2. Put some food on the edge of a chair seat. Cover, uncover … You got it!

3. Put a treat on your knee. Cover, uncover … dog backs off … reward.

Once she's got this, you can develop this into real life. You're eating a sandwich, and you "drop" a bit of bread on your knee. If your dog is staring at you eating this is a good time to teach her not to beg. Cover the bread quickly before she can lunge forward to snatch it. Uncover, cover, uncover till she backs off. Now you can remove the bread and carry on eating your sandwich. Do I reward her? Nope. If I do I'll be encouraging her staring and begging. *She needs to learn that staring at someone eating is never going to result in a reward.*

What I *will* do is some more Magic Hand training a bit later, when I'm not eating. Then she'll be well rewarded for leaving the food.

Science has proven that the cue (what kicks off the behaviour) becomes a reward in itself. As with any training, you start with massive and frequent rewards, then gradually lessen the number of rewards till what you're rewarding becomes a normal response. This may take hours, days, weeks, or even months, depending on the strength of your dog's begging and stealing, and the consistency with which you work. If she's been doing it for years, then it may take a little longer than with a young puppy. Remember, practice makes perfect! – with bad habits as well as good ones. All dogs are individuals with different learning speeds and experiences.

Consistency and clarity are the keys.

The more thorough you are at teaching this, the faster it will work and the faster you can assimilate it into daily life. You can start doing carefully-monitored set-ups similar to those in Lesson 3 Bringing the game to real life. You can leave a bit of food on the table where your dog can clearly see it, then busy yourself with something else in the room while keeping a close eye on proceedings.

If your dog stares at the food, you can go over and place your hand in front of it to protect it while your dog readjusts her mindset and changes her position, leaving the food alone.

If, while you're away from her, she makes a move to the food, try and resist the temptation to yell, "Ah-ah," "Noooo," or any of those other knee-jerk reactions you no longer need. Remember your own impulse control. I would probably say "Oh?" in a quiet voice, possibly followed by, "Is that really what you should be doing?" I know my dog doesn't understand the words, but she understands the interruption. She will appreciate the reminder and wiggle up to me saying, "I wasn't really going to take it, honest!"

An important word about words

There will come a time when you won't need to say or do anything. You can leave food wherever you want - a plate of hot dinner on the table, cakes on the coffee table, sandwiches on the picnic table - and it won't be touched. I habitually put my meal on the coffee table then go to fetch a glass of water. There are four dogs milling around, but I know my food will be untouched. Leaving food alone will become your dog's default behaviour.

But a vocal cue is useful - to remind your dog of impulse control when she comes across an unexpected bounty on the ground, or to suggest a calmer behaviour when she sees something exciting like a ball being kicked by some kids in the park.

So how do you connect your chosen word or words to your dog's action? Not having verbal language, your dog doesn't learn words in the same way we do. She learns by association. You describe what the dog is doing with your chosen word - your word is a label for that action. When you pair your puppy's name with a treat every time she responds, she knows that sound always means to come to you for good things. You are labelling the action of turning towards you and coming to you as "Millie!" Now you've got attention and the beginnings of a rock-solid recall.

How do we name this pulling away from a desired object? We do it by simply labelling that action just as she's doing it, and here's how.

Up to now you've been letting your Magic Hand do the talking, but when your dog's really good at this game you can start adding the cue. You can, of course, use any word or words you like - there are no rules! "Leave it" is a commonly used cue, but sadly it's often said in a menacing or furious manner - usually far too late - when the dog already has her jaws wrapped around whatever it is her owner wants her to leave. In other words, the poor dog has never been taught any of this and her owner expects her somehow to just know.

I use "Leave it," as you'll see in the following lesson. You can substitute whatever word you want, or use "Leave it". If you do, you must promise me that you won't turn into a hairy snarling monster when you say it! You say it calmly and quietly - as you would say Sit, Down, or Good Morning - you say it happily - as you would say "Millie!"

As with any word you use to ask your dog to do something, *you only say it once.* Repetition produces the opposite effect from what you want - it reduces responsiveness.

Lesson 4 Adding the cue

1. Start your Magic Hand game with your dog.

2. When she's backing off into her usual position every time, saying, "Ha! You can't catch me out," quietly add the words "Leave it" as she is making her move away.

3. Reward.

4. Repeat 2 and 3 till she's paired "Leave it" with her action of moving away.

5. Start saying, "Leave it" just before you expose the food.

6. When you can say, "Leave it," and get the thoughtful backing-off even without any temptation being visible, you'll know you've taught the cue right.

Troubleshooting

I'm guilty of yelling "Leave it!" Is my dog doomed now?

The joy of this way of working is that you always start from where you are and progress forward. What happened previously is of little importance. You may like to consider finding a new word, especially if you find yourself unable to say, "Leave it" nicely. You could even go so far as to use "No," as long as it's a conversational and lighthearted "Ooh no!" as opposed to a finger-wagging, bend-over-and-scowl, "Nooooooooooo!" If you do use "Leave it", be sure not to yell.

Lacy's Find

Here's a nice story for you, so you can see what you can expect!

I was playing with Lacy one day on a walk, throwing her frisbee for her - a quick game of speedy retrieves and returns to hand. As she was running back to me, a strong smell caught her by the nose. She stopped dead about 40 feet away from me, dropped her toy, and scooped something up from the ground. She tossed it in the air and caught it again. I called her as she picked *The Thing* up. I thought, "Well, she's swallowed whatever that was!" Leaving her beloved frisbee, she carried on running back to me and delivered to my hand a heap of fried chicken carcass discarded by a thoughtless picnicker. She hadn't eaten her find! She ran off again for her toy, I bagged and pocketed the bones, and we carried on playing.

Real-life Magic Hand at a distance.

In this section we have established:

- How to keep dropped or found food left where it is
- The safety advantages of this game
- Walks will become less stressful
- Words are not necessarily necessary
- "I prefer Mum's approval and a smidgin of hot dog to squashed chips on the road."

Chapter 4
Why does it work?

If facts and figures are anathema to you, skip to the next section. But if the nuts and bolts of human and animal behaviour interest you - why we actually do what we do - then read on.

People first

There is plenty of scientific proof concerning the principles of instant *versus* delayed gratification in humans, and it appears to me that it works just the same in your dog.

Sigmund Freud, back in 1911, argued that deferred gratification was a marker of increased maturity. Then Walter Mischel conducted his Marshmallow Test experiments at Stanford University in the late 1960s, on children between ages 3 and 5. In the Marshmallow Test, a child had to choose between eating one favourite treat straight away, or - if they could wait for 15 minutes - be rewarded with two treats. A small number of the children caved in straight away and settled for one treat. Of the remainder who chose to wait, only one third managed to last out the fifteen minutes and earn their double reward.

One of the findings was that if the researcher interacting with the child appeared inconsistent and broke promises, the child would lose faith in the new game and just take his one marshmallow while he could. This provides an interesting insight into our need as parents and dog-owners to be consistent and reliable - however busy or stressed we may be!

The detailed follow-up studies over the next 40 years were revealing. The children who, at 4, were able to delay gratification did better in school and university, were more successful, and enjoyed a more healthy lifestyle. The ability to make good choices is a predictor of a person's ability to make the best of their life. They can choose rational behaviour over desires - the pre-frontal cortex over the limbic system.

Cognitive Behavioural Therapy uses the "if-then" framework to help people overcome unwanted desires. "If this happens, then I move into that strategy." Repetition leads to new habits being formed.

Moving into specifically dog-focussed scientific work, the two pillars are Pavlov, the originator of Classical Conditioning, and B.F. Skinner, whose pioneering work with a broad range of animals resulted in Operant Conditioning being shown to be the best way to train any animal. We're animals too.

Pavlov's Dogs and Classical Conditioning

Classical Conditioning was first described by Ivan Pavlov (1849-1936). This area of study came as a by-product of his pioneering work on the digestive system for which he won a Nobel Prize in 1904. His work was far-reaching and forms the basis of what we know about digestion today.

But his name has been linked in the popular mind with one thing only – *Pavlov's Dogs*. In his study of the purpose and function of saliva, Pavlov used dogs in his laboratory. They were kept immobile, with drains collecting the saliva through fistulae in the dogs' necks. The objective was to collect the saliva for analysis when the dogs were fed. It was soon discovered, however, that the dogs would begin salivating increasingly earlier in the food preparation chain - first the sight of the lab technicians, then the sound of human activity, became enough to get the juices flowing in anticipation of their food.

Pavlov's genius was in interrupting this chain with a specific, non-food-linked sound. Amongst others, he chose his famous bell. The bell was rung before feeding, and after a few exposures, the dogs would begin to salivate at the sound of the bell - regardless of the time or other factors – and in the absence of food. Pavlov had effectively put the salivation (an unconditioned or spontaneous, unconsidered response) under stimulus control. Put another way, the bell cued the drooling. So by using a hitherto neutral stimulus (the bell) he could cause the salivation to occur without the normal, natural, unconditioned stimulus of the presence of food. The association that the bell signified food meant the bell would cue the drooling in the absence of food.

How does this apply to us?

With your own dog, you'll be able to see many examples of Classical Conditioning at work.

- Barking at the doorbell
- Leaping up at the sound of the car keys or when seeing you pick up the lead
- Appearing at your feet when you bang the dog bowl
- Rapt attention at the sound of the fridge door opening,
- or a plastic bag rustling,
- or the cat flap opening!

These sights or sounds all stimulate a response of excitement or salivation, even without the expected result of a visitor at the door, going for a walk, dinner, or the entry of the cat. This response has developed through continual repetition of a sequence which the dog anticipates.

You can see now where some of your dog's more annoying habits have come from, and how you can change them! Control the stimulus (the thing that's causing the reaction) and you control the outcome. In fact, if you remove the stimulus entirely - disconnect the doorbell, for instance - you can completely eliminate that response. Think about that!

Operant Conditioning

Operant Conditioning is the name given to the shaping system first described by B.F. Skinner (1904-1990) in 1938 in *The Behavior of Organisms.*

Skinner was influenced by Pavlov. Working largely with rats and pigeons, Skinner's work had a far-reaching effect on education and psychology. From a practical standpoint, it was used extensively in the American war effort in the forties. Dolphins were used for underwater work where it was unsafe for divers, and chickens became ace spotters - of life rafts in a choppy ocean far below the rescue plane - and of bombing targets.

It was developed and refined by the dolphin trainers who, after World War II, turned their attention to training animals for aquarium displays. The dolphin trainers introduced a marker. It's impossible to get a fish to a dolphin at the high point of a jump, so they marked the moment with a whistle, signalling the correct response from the animal and the imminent arrival of a fish. This whistle is a Secondary Reinforcer.

- A Primary Reinforcer is something that the subject finds innately reinforcing, such as food, play, or social interaction.
- A Secondary Reinforcer is found rewarding by the subject by its association with a Primary Reinforcer, for example money, tokens, whistle, clicker, or a marker word - "Yes!"

Operant Conditioning is so called because the subject has to decide to do something to achieve a reward - to operate on its environment. In Classical Conditioning, an action which occurs naturally is paired with a stimulus or cue. For example, offering your hand for the dog to touch: the dog comes to sniff your hand, then you add the cue. In Operant Conditioning the animal can make a choice of what behaviour to offer.

In a Skinner box - a small chamber for testing the responses of animals, often equipped with a food-producing mechanism - rats or pigeons could sleep, groom, run around, or press a lever which delivered food - a Primary Reinforcer. Skinner introduced Pavlov's discoveries by pairing a stimulus to the food delivery, so the subjects knew that touching the lever produced food. Naturally, touching the lever became very popular! When Skinner stopped rewarding the lever-pressing by failing to deliver food, after a flurry of repeated attempts and frustration the action died out entirely - an Extinction Burst.

Why does this matter to me and my pet dog?

The possibilities opened up by Operant Conditioning extend far beyond simply achieving a desired action. It has become a window into the animal's mind. Daily, we are extending our knowledge of how the critters think. The practical applications are boundless: in dogs alone we have mine detection, search and rescue, dogs for the disabled, hearing dogs for the deaf, seeing dogs for the blind, seizure alert medical assistance dogs, companion dogs, entertaining dogs, dancing dogs, agility dogs. A lot of the things these dogs can do would be very difficult, if not impossible, to teach by force, by luring, or by moulding the action - and there would be no enthusiasm and joy in the task!

Skinner's pioneering work, followed up and expanded by Marion Breland, Bob Bailey, and Karen Pryor amongst others, has enabled dogs to be used in so many of these new applications.

The important thing to remember with Operant Conditioning is that what you reinforce is what you get, so the timing of the reward is crucial! One moment you think you are capturing a wonderful Sit Pretty, but because you were too slow with the reward, you actually reinforced a floppy Sit. Remember the dolphins jumping: your marker means a reward. Clarity is key!

A word about punishment

Operant Conditioning has its own clearly defined language - Reinforcement or Punishment, Positive or Negative - which may not mean the same as is popularly perceived.

- Positive means adding or starting something
- Negative means taking something away or stopping it
- Reinforcement means to encourage what you want by rewarding it, making it more likely to happen again
- Punishment refers to punishing the behaviour, not the animal, making the action less likely to happen again. It does not necessarily include traditional punishments such as beating.

Put very briefly:

- Positive Reinforcement = Good starts
- Positive Punishment = Bad starts
- Negative Reinforcement = Bad stops
- Negative Punishment = Good stops

You don't need to remember all this - *just aim for Positive Reinforcement and reward what you like!*

If your dog does something you like, for instance, and you turn away and ignore her, this is punishing - discouraging the action. Imagine walking down the street, spotting someone you know, giving a cheery smile, and your acquaintance turns his head sharply away to walk past you without a word. How would you feel? What would you do next time you saw him on the street?

Skinner proved that if an action is rewarded, the subject is likely to repeat that action. Similarly, if an action is punished, the subject is unlikely to repeat it. How many times did you have to put your hand into the steam from a kettle before you stopped doing it? There is fallout from punishment, however, that eliminates its use from any humane training program. Obviously it causes unhappiness and pain, which should render it unacceptable to civilised people, but it also causes distrust, alienation, lying, and deceitful behaviour. If a child has been smacked for stealing a cake, he's going to make very sure he doesn't get caught while stealing the next one! It doesn't necessarily stop what you don't want - it may drive it underground.

Repeatedly rewarding what you do like will work much, much faster, and your dog's response will be durable - she'll always make the right choice. It is the element of choice that will transform your relationship with your dog, and - secret tip! - it works just the same with children, spouses, and work colleagues!

Think of the joy of never administering a telling-off ever again.

In this Chapter you've learnt that:

- People and dogs are much the same
- The research into the dog's mind is very advanced
- How you can adapt this knowledge for you and your pet
- "It's all Greek to me."

Chapter 5
Here comes the joy!

Rollo waits in front of the open door for permission to go out

The spin-off from teaching your dog impulse control with food can now be extended to impulse control with everything else. Here are twelve things for you to enjoy working on.

1. The Door

When you head to a door, do you get run over by a stampede as your dog crashes past your legs, bolting through the door as soon as it's opened a crack?

Let's change this, straight away:

1. Using the calm response you have taught with the Magic Hand Game, you head to the door and put your hand on the handle.

2. As your dog skids to a slippery halt and thuds into the closed door you ask for a Sit - only once. If you worked through the first book in this series Calm Down! Step-by-Step to a Calm, Relaxed, and Brilliant Family Dog you'll know that you can use your mat to help you here.

3. Once she sits, remove your hand from the door handle and toss a reward behind her so that she's up again.

4. Repeat, until your hand on the door handle causes her to sit without you needing to say it. This may take one or several short sessions depending on how good your timing is.

5. Once she sits every time you touch the door handle, you can start to turn the handle, but only as long as she stays sitting. Toss the treat away. If she jumps up, go back to Step 4.

6. Gradually your dog will learn to wait while you actually turn the handle without moving the door, then open the door a crack - this stage may take a while. But when you can open it a crack, keep working till you can open it fully while she sits - and waits. Huzzah!

7. Say your release word to send your dog through the door. You have got a release word, haven't you? I use "Break".

8. Advanced stuff: as she goes through the door, say Sit and she will turn, sit, and wait for you to come through, shut the door, and lock it.

2. The Car Door

Your dog will wait seated to get in the car, and - importantly for safety - she will wait till you "break" her to get out of the car, then sit beside you while you close the door and lock it.

1. Using the calm response you have taught with the Magic Hand, you head to the car with your dog on lead, and put your hand on the handle.

2. As your dog dances about waiting to hop in, you ask for a Sit - once. If you worked through the first book in this series, *Calm Down! Step-by-Step to a Calm, Relaxed, and Brilliant Family Dog,* you'll know that you can use your mat to help you here.

3. Once she sits remove your hand from the car door handle and toss a reward behind her so that she's up again.

4. Repeat, until your hand on the car door handle causes her to sit without you needing to say it. This may take one or several short sessions depending on how good your timing is.

5. Once she sits every time you touch the door handle, you can start to operate the handle. As long as she stays sitting, toss the treat away. If she jumps up, go back to Step 4.

6. Gradually your dog will learn to wait while you actually make that door-opening clunk with the handle without moving the door, then open the door a crack. As before, this stage may take a while, but keep working until you can open the door *fully* while she sits - and waits. Huzzah!

7. Say your release word to hop your dog up into the car. You have got a release word, haven't you? I use "Break."

8. Use the exact same sequence for releasing your dog from the car. You'll need to have her in a crate or you can lean in a side door to tether her so you don't slam the door on her head if she anticipates her release word.

9. You will be reaching in to clip a lead to her collar before releasing her, unhitching the fixed lead if you just tethered her. You may do

this several times in the sequence (clip on, clip off) so that she learns this is one of the stages she has to wait for.

10. Advanced stuff: Say "Sit" as she hops out of the car so she can spin round and sit beside you while you lock up the car.

3. The Crate

Does your dog have a crate or playpen? Use the same process for exit from the crate. Your hand on the crate latch will cause her to sit, then wait when the door is open till she's invited out to sit beside you.

1. Using the calm response you have taught with the Magic Hand, you head to the crate and put your hand on the latch.

2. Your snoozing dog will jump to attention. Open the crate door a crack, whoosh your arm in and give her a reward while sitting. Hold the treat up over her head so she has to be sitting to reach it. Shut the door and latch it again.

3. Repeat straight away until your hand on the door latch causes her to sit without you ever needing to say it. This may take one or several short sessions depending on how good your timing is.

4. Once she sits every time you touch the door latch, you can start to open the crate door a crack. As long as she stays sitting, give her a treat. If she jumps up or tries to bolt out of the crate, just close the door gently and go back to Step 3.

5. Gradually your dog will learn to wait while you open the door more widely. This stage may take a while, but continue to work until you can open it *fully* while she sits and waits. Huzzah!

6. Say your release word to let your dog come out of the crate. You have got a release word, haven't you? I use "Break".

7. Advanced stuff: as she comes through the door, say, "Sit," and she will turn, sit, and wait beside you - instead of hurtling off to follow her own agenda.

4. Furniture

How about hopping up on the furniture?

Maybe you let your dogs snooze in an armchair, or sit on your lap while you relax - I do - but that doesn't mean you have to put up with being landed on when you have a bowl of soup on your lap! And it certainly doesn't mean that you may not sit in your own armchair because your dog is in it.

Using the same system of impulse control, my dogs will sit beside me and "ask" to get on my lap. If I want that, I'll invite them to hop up. It took no time for my puppy to realise that leaping up unbidden resulted in landing on the floor again, while sitting patiently got him the cuddle he wanted.

The Magic Hand system taught him that nagging doesn't work, while patient waiting at a polite distance does.

1. Your dog is about to leap onto your lap.

2. Hold up your hand like a policeman.

3. Ask her calmly, "What do you think you should do now?" Remember that interacting with your dog does not need to include yelling, "Gerroff! SIT!"

4. *Wait* for her to give an appropriate response. The first time out it may be just to stand and wait. You can reward this stage by inviting her up.

5. Next time you can *wait* for her to give you a Sit before inviting her up.

My dogs are welcome to use my chair when I'm not in it, as long as they hop off as I approach it.

1. Dog is snoozing in your chair - that's fine - but you want to sit there.

2. Move purposefully towards the chair.

3. Dog stays put.

4. Lower yourself carefully into the chair and slowly lean back.

5. By now your dog will have hopped off.

6. In future, just advancing on the chair will be enough to let your dog know she should move.

Serious note: If you get any growling or nastiness, this is indicative of a larger problem of Resource Guarding and you need to find a force-free trainer straight away to help you. Do not get bitten!

5. Toy Play

Playing tug is a great way to teach your puppy Impulse Control

Playing exciting games with your dog is the key to building a terrific partnership, but just like our games, games with your dog need structure and boundaries.

Playing tennis with a friend would be no fun if he insisted on standing on the same side of the net as you, or simply hit all the balls over the fence. All our games have rules and structure. So you decide on the rules of play with your dog. Basically my rules are simple: my dog should not snatch the toy from my hand, grab my sleeve, or leap up and bite my nose; she should give the toy up when I want it back, and she should not dodge about just out of reach.

Use your Magic Hand principle:

1.   Hold out the toy. If she tries to grab it, the toy disappears behind your back until she waits calmly. When you bring it out, she continues to wait calmly till it's offered to her. If she tries to grab it, it goes back behind your back again. Run through this quickly.

2.   When she's clearly not jumping it's Game On: you whack the toy on the floor or hold it out to her saying, "Geddit!"

3.   To get the toy back, either put a treat to her nostrils or relax your pull on the toy and wait for her to let go - give the treat and start again; or, if she's pulling like a maniac and has no interest in the treat, *gently* hold her collar still so she can no longer pull while you relax your pull on the toy till she's so bored she lets go.

Either way, it's her choice to keep to these rules.

If your puppy is over the top, snatchy and bitey, she's probably too tired. She needs a break in her crate for a good sleep before the next game.

6. Reclaiming Stolen Shoes

Your dog has grabbed something you value and crouched into a playbow to invite you to chase her. Don't! If you do, you'll be playing her favourite game - forever.

1. Feign complete indifference about the article she has, get a tasty treat, offer it to her then close your hand over it. Magic Hand again. Now she's going to move into that state of mind which requires thinking in order to get the treat: "Ah! I know this game."

2. When she decides to wait politely, offer the treat to her with your other hand. She'll drop the precious item into your waiting hand so she can enjoy her treat. This can all be done without any shouting or histrionics from you.

3. Now get one of her own toys, chuck it for her, and enjoy a game.

4. And put your shoes away! Don't make life hard for yourself - or your puppy.

7. Mugging Your Hand or Your Pocket for Those Treats

Treat training can result in unwanted pestering or "mugging." Of course you'll never reward or reinforce mugging or begging by feeding your dog now, will you?

Mugging is the last thing we want, so encourage your dog to use her new-found impulse control to refrain from this practice.

1. Your dog is staring at your pocket, or nosing or nudging your hand for treats.

2. Turn so that your pocket is inaccessible, or clasp your treat-filled hands to your chest. Keep still and wait. This may be enough for her to realise her mistake and desist.

3. If necessary you can add, "What should you be doing right now?"

4. If neither of these is reaching your determined dog's mind, gently and silently slip your hand in her collar to lower her front feet to the ground - or hold her away from the pocket while she collects herself.

5. Tell her she's good and go about your business.

6. Soon you can ask her to do something and reward her. She needs to know that treats come as a result of doing something you like. It's up to her to work out what this may be!

7. Don't keep treats on your person. Have containers of treats strategically placed around the house so you can always catch and reward something good. They should be within easy reach - for you, but not for her!

8. Tasty Shopping Bags in the Car

1. Teach your dog that plastic bags are not fair game. You can do this in the kitchen.

2. Put the bag of goodies on the floor, quietly say, "Leave it," and reward your dog for leaving the bag of goodies alone.

3. Repeat a few times.

4. Now put the bag in the car and repeat.

5. Bags in the car will now earn the same respect.

Many years ago I had a small Whippet cross and a very large German Shepherd. Poppy had been leaving food bags in the car alone for years. When Corin, the huge young German Shepherd, went to stick his nose in a shopping bag, Poppy rumbled menacingly - thinking, "If anyone's going to get that food it'll be me!" Corin clearly decided that shopping bags were very dangerous, and forever after would plaster himself to the furthest part of the car when shopping bags were there. You can achieve the same effect with no growling!

9. Helping Tidy Up the Kitchen (aka Countersurfing)

Countersurfing is the annoying habit some dogs develop of cruising the kitchen worktops - either with two feet or all four! - scavenging any crumb, smear, chocolate cake, or rump steak that they may find.

First things first: if you don't want your dog to practice a bad habit then you must ensure that she has no opportunity to do so. So no food - crumbs count as food - may be left on the kitchen counters, and *never* leave her in the kitchen unattended.

Then use your Magic Hand.

1. Remember the food on the floor sequence? If your dog's nose appears in front of some food you're preparing, there's no need to yell or dance. Just put your hand in front of the food, giving her a moment to process this information - then she'll drop her feet to the floor again.

2. Reward her for a little distance and when she's not begging.

For an ongoing counter-countersurfing program, you can't beat Impulse Control combined with Matwork. Fortunately there's a book in this series, *Calm Down! Step-by-step to a Calm, Relaxed, and Brilliant Family Dog* - more info in the Resources section - which will take you step-by-step to having a calm and relaxed dog who goes to her mat and lies down whenever you start preparing food.

What about on walks?

10. Marking Every Tree

Not confined to males, this is often allowed to develop because people think it's a normal dog activity. Not really. My dogs can mark whatever they like on their own time, but if they're walking with me ... they walk with me. In my mind, walking excludes hauling me towards every lamp-post to check the pee-mail. Allow your dog one opportunity to relieve herself. After that, she's walking with you. No marking.

Another book in this series - *Let's Go! Enjoy Companionable Walks with your Brilliant Family Dog* (info in the Resources Section) - will take you step-by-step to achieving calm and comfortable walks with your dog. Along with Impulse Control you have a winning combination!

But for now, you can engage your dog in conversation whenever a likely tree or lamp-post hoves into view. Congratulate her warmly for focussing on you as you walk blithely by. Remember always to reward anything she does that you like!

11. Passing Quietly By Previously Exciting Things

Your dog does not need to drag you excitedly towards every living being (or inert or dead thing) she sees on the street. Teaching her impulse control will spread into her everyday life so that she can view things more calmly and make better decisions.

If she's desperate to examine something, you can ask her for attention first, then give her permission to "Go sniff!" There's lots more about this in The Premack Principle which you'll find in a little while.

This system also leads to calm greetings when you want your dog to meet someone or another dog.

12. Meet and Greet Nicely

This is a large subject that I will only touch on here. If your dog is one of those that gets over-the-top excited at the sight of a person (heaven!) or another dog (wowee!!) - common in young sociable pups - you can help keep things calm by eliciting a bit of self-control before they are permitted to greet the object of their desire.

1. Wait for a Sit, or just eye contact, from your dog before giving permission to greet. I give permission by saying, "Go say Hi!"

2. You can interrupt the greeting by calling her back for a treat, then - if things are going well - she can greet again.

See *Let's Go! Enjoy Companionable Walks with your Brilliant Family Dog* for some cracking lead skills. Once you have these skills down, you never have to pull your dog's lead again. Really - never again!

The Premack Principle

This principle was first defined by the psychologist David Premack. For us, it simply means that your dog will choose to do something a bit dull or non-rewarding, such as sitting still in the face of temptation, in order to get something which is exciting and rewarding.

Think of a family situation where the children may watch television (very rewarding) as soon as they've put their things away (very, very boring). Kids will race with enthusiasm to bundle everything up and stuff it in a cupboard so they can get to their beloved tv. You can use the same principle with your dog, and it's all impulse control!

The greeting example in *12. Meet and Greet Nicely* above used Premack to teach your dog to choose to sit (boring) - difficult when she is desperate to bounce on a visitor - in order to get the release "Go say Hi!" (wonderful!)

Another way I use Premack to get nice walking on the lead from my pups is this:

1. You're walking your young dog and you come to a grassy area beside the path which screams, "Sniff me!"

2. Your pup lunges towards it, but you keep on walking by.

3. When you've passed the spot, you can turn and walk back again.

4. Your pup lurches out again - keep walking.

5. After you've walked by the enticing grassy patch a few times, your dog will twig that she's not to pull you about and walk nicely with you.

6. The split second she does that, you can turn to the grass and say, "Go sniff!"

So she learns that walking nicely on the lead will buy her the opportunity to sniff exciting things.

Only do this once or twice on a walk with your young dog, otherwise she's going to think she can sniff every other blade of grass as long as she walks past with you first.

In this section we have established that:

-   Impulse Control rules!
-   You can apply this to many different areas of your daily life with your dog
-   Your dog is so much cleverer than you thought!
-   "I'm so much cleverer than you thought!"

Chapter 6
The effect of Impulse Control
on the two of you

*The doughnuts are quite safe from Cricket the Whippet,
even without being reminded*

So how is this all going to affect your daily life with your dog?

What effect will this have on my dog?

First of all impulse control will give your dog a wonderful feeling of freedom.
Impulse Control is empowering! In the same way that people "grow into" a

senior role when promoted, you can watch your dog blossom as she learns to apply these principles to the whole of her life. Once you can trust her not to chew up the carpets or steal the sandwiches you can give her much more freedom. She can - in time - have the run of the house and garden without endangering the furniture, the fittings, the plants, the lawn, or any food left *anywhere*.

The trust you show in her will build her trust in you. Whenever she leaves anything tempting alone you must be sure to observe and reward her with whatever reward is suitable - from a smile or stroke to a treat or game. Her confidence will grow. She knows what she has to do and what is expected of her. *This clarity leads to self-confidence.* A dog who doesn't know what she's meant to do is forever looking over her shoulder wondering if she's going to be yelled at for some unknown transgression.

Your dog will become more patient, more thoughtful, and more reflective. This response will spread to every area of her life - and this response builds with experience.

In a multi-dog household new pups copy their elders. A useful spin-off is that your new puppy will now have excellent mentors to emulate and will learn much faster. Because there is a lack of confusion and your dog is clear on her boundaries, the general excitement level in the household is lowered. Instead of reacting to everything that occurs, your dog can take much more in her stride.

Will your dog pester you for food? No. She knows that begging and mugging is not rewarded. She knows she can earn rewards by pleasing you. This does depend on you being free with your praise and rewards - there's no place for miserliness here.

You make a deal with your dog: you do what I want and you'll get what you want.

Don't break that deal!

So how will all this affect me?

You don't have to keep everything you value under lock and key. You can take your lunch out to the garden and leave it on the picnic table – like the plate of doughnuts in the picture above - while you come back into the house for your drink or book. Instead of hairy sharks wheeling round the table waiting for their moment to strike, your dogs will pass no comment on this plate of goodies and it will be safe till you return.

If you take your dinner into the tv room, leaving it on the coffee table, it will still be there, untouched, when you come back. You can kick off your shoes and know that they will not be chewed or loved. If your young dog feels the need to chew, she knows where her toy box is and can help herself to one of her own chewies. Shopping bags with meat and cakes can be left on the floor waiting to be unpacked without wet noses rooting around in them. Like the bag containing the pork chops which was left on the floor by the fridge for hours the other day because of a distraction. The pork chops remained untouched all afternoon by the four dogs.

This is the same that we teach and expect of our children - only dogs learn way faster!

Your home is calmer. You are calmer. You trust your dog. You will be more patient - you too will learn impulse control! You'll know that shouting and frustration have no place in a mature relationship, and that just waiting for the desired response is enough. You honour your dog. You respect your dog. No longer is she a nuisance-mutt who needs to be restrained and whose base impulses need to be kept at bay.

Mutual trust

This mutual trust leads to a greater bond between you and your dog. Your companion can truly share her life with you. You know where you are with her. She can become the brilliant family dog you always wanted! When I put on my jumper there's likely to be a cascade of treats tumbling from the pocket and bouncing across the floor. Four dogs watch this with interest. Do they plunge in to hoover up the spilt treats as fast as possible? Nope. They wait. I clear up the dropped treats - but they each get one for their self-control and mature responsibility.

You've probably already been astonished by how quickly your dog learnt the Magic Hand trick.

I was working with an impulsive terrier who was in sore need of self-control. When I explained what I was about to teach him, his owners said, "That won't work for Dodger. He'll never give up trying to get the food out of your hand. He'll just keep on biting and digging." In a very short time - shorter than usual, in fact - their little dog was backing off politely from my hand to wait patiently for his reward. I think the owners' jaws are still dropped!

So how quickly can this spread to the rest of your dog's life? It really all depends - not on your dog - but on you. How consistent can you be? How calm and patient? How reliable are you? Remember the children in the Marshmallow Test who would not trust their researcher if he showed himself to be unreliable? If he couldn't keep a deal, why should they?

We only have our dogs for a short time - far too short. There is no time allowance for damaging and breaking your relationship. There is no point in trying to make a point.

Enjoy the simplicity of working with your dog on a choice and reward basis.

Life has just become so easy!

Side effects

And there's much more!

See this: once your dog has learnt to control herself around food, she can adapt this to controlling herself around other exciting things in her life -

squirrels, birds, other dogs, children running, balls, other dogs' toys, [*insert your dog's most exciting thing here!*]

You don't have to cover the other dogs or children with your hand! You appeal to the same reflective side of her nature to get her to think through a problem to figure out an appropriate reaction. Instead of the current, "SQUIRRELS!!!" and a full-speed hurtle towards them - deaf to your protests - you can get her to pause and think. If you like her calm response and the area is safe, you could consider sending her after the squirrels as a reward. Don't worry - the squirrels will always get away up the nearest tree! The thrill of speed and the chase is the reward.

So instead of the backing off signal, turning away her head, or whatever your dog was doing with the food in your hand or on the floor, you can ask for a Sit and eye contact before being given permission to greet a visitor, run towards another dog, chase a rabbit - or whatever it may be.

It may not be appropriate for the thing she wants to be a reward. So you'll have others up your sleeve - good treats or a favourite toy - so you can reward her for engaging with you, then keep that engagement as you move away from the distraction.

You are aiming for your dog to be able to respond to you when she's highly aroused by some deep instinctive drive. This is hard for her! It may take some time before she's able to do this - but she'll never be able to do it if you don't teach her.

Racing off impetuously can have tragic results, of course, if there happens to be a road between her and The Exciting Thing. It can also be a nuisance or cause trouble - knocking over a small child, for instance, or crashing into a dog that does not welcome attention.

You'll need a cast-iron recall too, see *Here Boy! Step-by-step to a Stunning Recall from your Brilliant Family Dog* - the fourth book in this series of Essential Skills for a Brilliant Family Dog. More information is available in the Resources section of this book.

Coco the miniature poodle pup adores people. He gets wildly excited at the sight of a new victim for his attentions. He sings, he dances, he pirouettes, and he waves his paws, but he's learning that no greeting will ever take place without quiet and stillness from him first. So the sight of an oncoming person is beginning to produce a Sit from him and a distracted gaze at me, with only very quiet squeaking while he waits for his permission to, "Go say Hi!" This will gradually improve until all the anticipatory noise is eliminated, and he can sit - genuinely calmly - in the presence of new people.

Remember in Chapter 5, *1. The Door* where your hand on the door handle produced a sit, resulting in the opening of the door? This is a similar game - only with far greater stimulation and distraction! The sight of The Desired Object is a cue for your dog to sit.

When I call my whippet Cricket off a bunny chase I can see the strong battle going on in her head, and I can see her joy when she makes a good choice. This is a result of strengthening her "decision-making muscles" in the face of the food temptation. Those muscles are now strong enough to resist the instinctive drive of a whippet to chase rabbits - what she was bred for.

If you can use impulse control to call a sighthound off a rabbit-chase - you're doing well! There is, of course, a strong recall here - more of that in *Here Boy! Step-by-step to a Stunning Recall from your Brilliant Family Dog* – the fourth book in this series.

That's mine!

Another area where Impulse Control can be of great help is that of Resource Guarding.

Resource Guarding is when your dog seriously guards something she values - usually by freezing, keeping her head low over the item, showing the whites of her eyes, wrinkling her lips, maybe snarling, growling, snapping, and if challenged, biting.

The thing she values could be food, a dead bird, a toy, a twig, a tissue, her bed, the car - or you. Or any number of other things she prizes.

If the Resource Guarding is *very, very mild,* opening and closing your Magic Hand in front of her can move her into that mental space where she stops reacting and starts thinking rationally. If this is the case, she can drop the item into your hand for you to admire and return to her, or to swap for a high-value similar object or a treat. Never try and snatch away the thing she's guarding.

You are not "climbing down" or "losing face." It's not about you. It's about changing your dog's perception of this attack on her in the most painless way possible - and the most effective way!

This will build her trust in you that you won't take away her prized thing, rather you'll reward her for letting you look at it and sometimes swap it for something else equally as good. Exchange is no robbery.

IMPORTANT WARNING: If the resource guarding is extreme or well established, and your dog is showing any of the signs in the list above, then you should not attempt anything at home, but immediately find yourself an experienced professional force-free trainer or behaviourist who will give you a program to safely manage then change this habit.

Never challenge a dog who is guarding something - you are likely to get bitten.

It's all tricks to them

20-week-old puppy Lulu waits patiently while I pile cheese onto her paws.

Let's move to an area where your dog's impulse control really comes into its own: Tricks! Combine impulse control with your dog's creativity and you'll both have great fun with them. There are some great tricks you can teach your dog which involve resisting temptation. People will marvel at what your clever dog can do! Remember that when teaching something you should focus on teaching and not testing.

Food on The Paws

Once you've gone through the steps of the Magic Hand with food on the floor in Chapter 3, Lesson 2, you're ready to teach your dog the trick of lying down with food on each paw - and leaving it alone!

1. You're covering and uncovering the food under your hand till your dog will give you her "Hallo, it's this zen thing again" action immediately, so you can reward her. Remember: She never gets the food that she's leaving; she gets food from your other hand.

2. Repeat Step 1 but gradually get your hand-and-food combo closer and closer to your dog's paws with each repetition until your hand is

touching her paw.

3. The next move will be to place the food on one of her paws and immediately cover it, uncover it, and so on.

4. When she's showing that she won't touch the food, you take it off her paw and offer her a treat from your other hand.

5. Once this one-paw trick is perfected, you can build this up to food on both paws.

6. And once your dog can do this trick for you in any room in the house you can try showing it off to your friends - who will be astonished!

Troubleshooting

My dog is doing this brilliantly till I put the food on her paw, then she snatches her foot away.

Some dogs have really tickly feet! Try handling her feet gently for a reward at other times in the day so she gets used to the sensation being a good thing. When you put the food on her paw use a firmer hand-touch and press the food gently onto her paw.

We were going great but she snatched the food up.

Don't take your hand away completely until you're sure she won't take the food. Also, keep it very quick to begin with. You can gradually add a little duration to this trick as you go along, but *don't leave your poor dog nailed to the floor by cheese cubes for long!*

Food on the Head

Once you've got the Food on the Paws trick perfected, you can go for an advanced trick. Keep in mind, this is harder for your dog because you have to get the food onto her head while she's trying to look up and see what you're doing with it!

1. Having her in a Down first may make this learning a bit easier.

2. You may need to get her focussing on the treats on her paws first so you can place the food on her head very, very gently without disturbing her.

3. Very carefully place a piece of cheese on her head. She may not even realise it's there - but it looks good!

4. Over time you can work on the head-food without the paw-food.

The Famous Tossing the Biscuit off the Nose Trick

You can build up to this trick. It's well-known, but surprisingly difficult for the dog. The trick involves placing a small biscuit, piece of cheese, or sausage on your dog's nose. She has to wait till you release her, then she can have it.

This will go through a few stages before you get the desired final trick.

1. You may have to ask your dog to place her chin on your palm so that her head stays level - otherwise the treats will be rolling off her nose all over the place!

2. When she's happy with that - don't forget to reward this new mini-trick! - you can hold the treat on her muzzle, just on the edge of the nose-leather is the best place. She'll go comically cross-eyed trying to look at it!

3. Remove that treat and give it to her.

4. She may still be resting her chin on your other hand, but slowly and gradually build up through the stages so that you can remove your

hand from the treat for a split second, then a second, then a little longer before you give her the treat. Eventually, remove your chin-support. Reward each step. Have fun with her!

5.   Finally add your "Geddit!" cue so she can get the treat. She may well just tip her head so the treat falls on the floor. Enjoy her triumph and repeat the sequence on another day till she's really got it.

6.   She'll start to pull her head away quickly and snatch the treat out of the air.

Have fun with this and you can impress your friends with her incredible Impulse Control!

In this Chapter we have established that:

- Having Impulse Control will change your dog's life
- It will also change your life
- You'll develop mutual trust
- A bit about Resource Guarding
- How to teach some great foodie tricks
- "I'm going cross-eyed staring at this cheese on my nose!"

Conclusion
You are a huge way into your journey!

If you've followed me through this book step by step, you'll now have a dog who can be trusted around food - whether found, dropped, or left out on a table or counter - and you'll be well on the way to having a dog who can contain her excitement in the face of her greatest challenges - children, people, other dogs, a moving ball or bike …

Or maybe you work like me and you've had a read-through first, so you know where you're going with this, and you're now ready to go back, read the book again and start the learning with your dog. There are just four skills you need to turn your wild puppy into your Brilliant Family Dog. Just four. Everything else flows from these. If you have these four skills - you're done!

You have in this book one quarter of what you need to have a Brilliant Family Dog. To find the other three parts, have a look at the Resources section at the end of this book.

Appreciation

I want to offer thanks to all those who have helped me get where I am with my dogs:

- First of all, my own long-suffering dogs! They have taught me so much when I've taken the time to listen.

- My students, who have shown me how they learn best, enabling me to give them what they need to know in a way that works for them.

- Some legendary teachers, principal amongst them: Sue Ailsby, Leslie McDevitt, Grisha Stewart, Susan Garrett. I wholeheartedly recommend them. They are trailblazers.

Resources

If you've enjoyed learning this key skill and you want to find the other three parts of the puzzle, go to www.brilliantfamilydog.com/books and pick up your next book!

Calm Down! *Step-by-Step to a Calm, Relaxed, and Brilliant Family Dog - Book 1*

Let's Go! *Enjoy Companionable Walks with your Brilliant Family Dog - Book 3*

Here Boy! *Step-by-Step to a Stunning Recall from your Brilliant Family Dog - Book 4*

These cover the four skills you need to turn your wild puppy into your Brilliant Family Dog.

And if you've got any specific queries, you can email me direct at beverley@brilliantfamilydog.com This will come straight to my personal inbox and I'll answer you - usually within 48 hours. Try me!

Meanwhile, for more free training, go to www.brilliantfamilydog.com and get a series of instructional emails on common day-to-day problems, like jumping up, chewing, barking, and so on.

Thank you for the insightful emails - we are applying the techniques and find the information really helpful. *Lucy and Ted*

I just wanted to say how much I enjoy your emails. I nearly always learn something new and they also remind me of ways to encourage good behaviour and therefore promote everyday enjoyment for both my dogs and myself! *Amanda and Ella*

Thank you for the emails, they are a great source of information. *Simon and Murphy*

Thank you for all these brilliant tips! *Shabra and Archi*

I've found your tips extremely interesting, helpful and above all really generous of you. Thank you. *Shelley and Jesse*

Works consulted for Chapter 4

http://www.britannica.com/biography/Sigmund-Freud accessed 2015

Mischel, W., et al. (1989). *Delay of gratification in children.* Science, 24 4 (4907), 933–938

https://www.apa.org/helpcenter/willpower-gratification.pdf accessed 2015

Casey, B. J., et al. (2011). *Behavioral and neural correlates of delay of gratification 40 years later.* Proceedings of the National Academy of Sciences, 10 8 (36), 14998–15003

http://www.nobelprize.org/nobel_prizes/medicine/laureates/1904/pavlov-bio.html accessed 2015

http://psychology.about.com/od/classicalconditioning/a/pavlovs-dogs.htm accessed 2015

Skinner, B.F. (1938) *The Behavior of Organisms: An Experimental Analysis*, New York; Appleton-Century

Skinner, B.F. (1951) *"How to teach animals"* Scientific American

Reynolds, G.S. (1968), *A Primer of Operant Conditioning.* Palo Alto, California: Scott, Foresman

Bailey, B, and M.B. Bailey (1996) *Patient Like the Chipmunks.* Eclectic Science Productions

http://www.clickertraining.com/karen accessed 2015

Mary R. Burch and Jon S. Bailey (1999), *How Dogs Learn*, Wiley, NY

Free Training for you!

Jumping up?

Barking?

Chewing?

Get inventive solutions to everyday problems with your dog

www.brilliantfamilydog.com

About the author

I've been training dogs for many years. First for competitive dog sports and over time to be stellar family pets. For most of my life, I've lived with up to four dogs, so I'm well used to getting a multi-dog household to run smoothly. It soon became clear that a force-free approach was by far the most successful, effective, and rewarding for me and the dogs. I've done the necessary studying for my various qualifications - for rehab of anxious and fearful "aggressive" dogs, early puppy development, and learning theory and its practical applications. I am continually studying and learning this endlessly amazing subject!

There are some superb teachers and advocates of force-free dog training, and you'll find those I am particularly indebted to in the Resources Section. Some of the methods I show you are well-known in the force-free dog training community, while many have my own particular twist.

A lot of my learning has come through the Puppy Classes, Puppy Walks, and Starter Classes I teach. These dog-owners are not looking for competition-standard training; they just want a Brilliant Family Dog they can take anywhere. Working with real dogs and their real owners keeps me humble - and resourceful! It's no good being brilliant at training dogs if you can't convey this enthusiasm and knowledge to the person the dog has to live with. So I'm grateful for everything my students have taught me about how they learn best.

Beverley Courtney BA(Hons) CBATI CAP2 MAPDT(UK) PPG

CPSIA information can be obtained
at www.ICGtesting.com
Printed in the USA
LVHW010401010821
694234LV00021B/1955